Pastor Search Committee Planbook

Pastor Search Committee Planbook

GERALD M. WILLIAMSON

BROADMAN
&HOLMAN
PUBLISHERS

Nashville, Tennessee

ISBN: 978-0-8054-3515-3

Dewey Decimal Classification: 254

Subject Heading: PASTOR SEARCH COMMITTEE

Library of Congress Catalog Card Number:
81-68923

Printed in the United States of America

FLOWCHART OF USE OF RESOURCE KIT

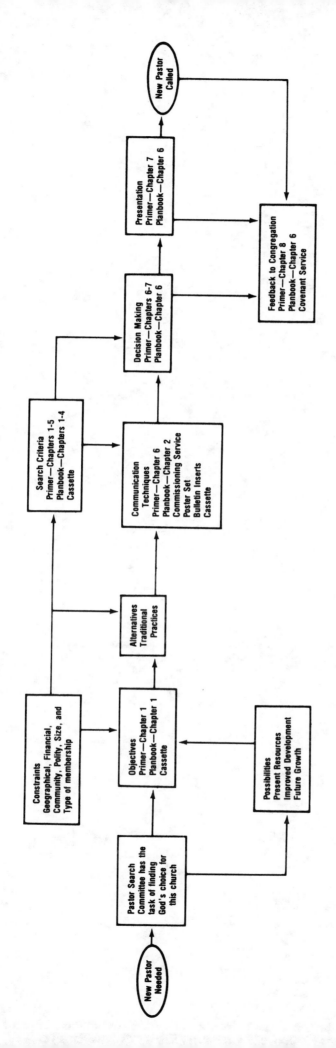

New Pastor Needed

Pastor Search Committee has the task of finding God's choice for this church

Constraints
Geographical, Financial, Community, Polity, Size, and Type of membership

Objectives
Primer—Chapter 1
Planbook—Chapter 1
Cassette

Possibilities
Present Resources
Improved Development
Future Growth

Alternatives
Traditional Practices

Search Criteria
Primer—Chapters 1-5
Planbook—Chapters 1-4
Cassette

Communication Techniques
Primer—Chapter 6
Planbook—Chapter 2
Commissioning Service
Poster Set
Bulletin Inserts
Cassette

Decision Making
Primer—Chapters 6-7
Planbook—Chapter 6

Presentation
Primer—Chapter 7
Planbook—Chapter 6

New Pastor Called

Feedback to Congregation
Primer—Chapter 8
Planbook—Chapter 6
Covenant Service

COMMITTEE OFFICERS

Chairperson _____

Vice-Chairperson _____

Secretary _____

Contents

Introduction

Before All Else Fails Read These Directions

The whole intent of this book is to assist each member of the Pastor Search Committee to act with confidence in the quest of the committee goal. While the trial-and-error method of doing a job has some value, it should not have to be the primary technique used by a Pastor Search Committee.

A logical and chronological approach will enable the Pastor Search Committee to keep all matters in proper perspective. Negative forces such as disinterest, discontent, disharmony, and panic should not be telling factors.

Assumptions Must Precede Directions

The directions for using this book are positive and written with a sense of expectancy. This is so because they and the whole book are based on these assumptions:

1. The church which has elected this Pastor Search Committee did so under the will of God and direction of the Holy Spirit.

2. Each member of the committee has agreed to serve based upon personal soul-searching and prayer which led to the conclusion that it is indeed God's will that this personal service be given.

3. The church, the committee as a whole, and each person on the committee is committed to praying continually for God's leadership in the work being done and for his will in the ultimate call of the pastor.

It is acknowledged that not every church, committee, or person involved is going to be as fervently dedicated to the truths of these assumptions as they should. However, the use of this book and the related materials will help all concerned grow closer to being in tune with the previously enumerated assumptions.

Six Basic Directions for Using This Book

1. The book is devised with two types of sessions which the committee should use.

A. *Study sessions*—the primary purpose of the study sessions is to think about your progress to that point, examine your needs for continuing to make headway, and set your plans for completing that next step.

B. *Development sessions*—in these, the committee takes the skills acquired in previous study sessions and uses them. For example, after studying methods of screening prospects, the members set aside a session to spend in actually screening.

2. The suggested agenda for each session should be followed unless there is strong reason not to do so. It sets the pattern for effectively pulling together the various resources in the total kit. It is also planned to conserve time by keeping the whole committee moving in the same direction.

3. *Objectives*—Each person reads the objective at the appropriate time on the agenda. When a committee member does not feel comfortable with a statement, time is taken to assist the person(s).

4. *Assignments*—These are the glue for the framework that is being constructed each session. A committee cannot possibly do all of its work within the time limits of the group sessions. Tasks must be allotted to individuals or subcommittees.

Ordinarily, the assignments are related to the subject of the session. Where it is beneficial to the progress of the committee, advance research is suggested.

5. *Reproduction of materials*—All parts of this book and the kit as a whole are copyrighted. Permission is given for copying forms and questionnaires for one-time use only.

Additional supplies are available where the original sources were purchased.

6. *Timing of sessions*—You are encouraged to keep an eye on the clock. In fact, a good investment will be the purchase of a kitchen timer which can be set over and over. Use it to help keep you on the time schedules suggested throughout this book.

Developing an Information Foundation for the Pastor Search Committee

First: Know what you need to study as a committee and how you should spend your early sessions. (See objectives.)

Second: Begin to gather and correlate information from the congregation and the committee which delineates the type of pastor desired. (See survey and priority scale.)

Third: Begin now to use the tools (ideas, methods, materials, books, cassettes) which you find. It is a mistake "to plan to use them" because the habit of doing without easily develops.

Fourth: Determine the way in which you will evaluate your efforts during the time you function as a committee. (See "checklist" in *Primer* appendix as one possible resource.)

Fifth: Take the time to formally adopt as a committee the policies and procedures which are to be officially followed. Relate these as soon as possible to the congregation.

1

Expanding the Views
of Your Tasks

Study Session 1—
Building a Plan for Action

Agenda:
Becoming acquainted with one another
Determining what you are going to be
Ascertaining the steps to be followed
Discovering how closely your thinking
relates to that of the others of the
committee
Making assignments for orderly progress
Praying for leadership

Objectives:
Upon completion of this session—
1. You will have a new appreciation
for the dedication of the other committee
members.
2. You will have decided upon a name
for your committee which reflects its purpose.
3. You will be able to see beyond your
personal perceptions and have knowledge of the consensus of the committee
as to the priorities of time for your "pastor-to-be."
4. You will be beginning to achieve a
spiritual bond with the other members of
the committee.

Becoming Acquainted with One Another
(15-45 min.)
"I didn't know that about you" was the
response of every person present when
Mr. Trueblood shared that he had only
been a Christian for two years when he
had transferred his membership to Trinity Church. Several of them had been
contemplating nominating him as chairman of the committee. They now felt the
need to give the matter more consideration even though he had natural leadership abilities.

They were still thinking about this
when they realized that Mrs. Stone was
talking in an animated fashion. After experiencing several outbursts of laughter,
most of the committee realized that they
had no previous inkling of Mrs. Stone's
sense of humor. Subconsciously they
expressed gratitude for this unexpected
gift to what could be long and extended
meetings.

You don't really know all you think
you do about the people who are going
to be with you a great deal in the coming
weeks. Time spent in gettting acquainted
in the context of this particular group
(Pastor Search Committee) will be of immense value for the future.

Some suggested topics are included.
Choose one (or more) according to the
depth of past relationships. They are arranged in order from "well acquainted"
to "didn't you just join our church last
year?" A two-minute limit should be observed.

1. Each one tell something about another member of your family which is

probably not known by the majority of the group.

Examples: "I have a brother who is a minister of music in Illinois" or "My father was a deacon in the same church for thirty-five years" or "My son went to the state university on a basketball scholarship before we moved here six years ago."

2. Every member of the committee share about a key concern you have for the church. No one can say, "Mine is the same."

Examples: "We are becoming an increasingly aging church, but we do not give attention to the aging members of our congregation" or "The young adult families of our church seem to be having many problems, but no one is giving them any special attention" or "The maintenance problems of our church are growing each year, but we are just troubleshooting instead of trying to find long-range solutions."

3. One by one members ask one other member two questions that would be helpful in getting acquainted.

Examples: "Where were you living when you became a Christian?" or "What kind of work do you do?" or "What are your hobbies or special interests outside of your vocation?" or "Where did you receive your education?" or "What jobs have you held in the churches where you have been a member?" or "What would you like to do that you have not done?"

Even a small committee will need to keep some time limitation on the answers to these questions, and large committees will find it an imperative.

One other question should be used by every Pastor Search Committee. A little more freedom of time should be given on this one since it is a two-part question.

"What were your first feelings when you were informed you had been elected to this committee; and what changes of feeling have you experienced since the committee was formed?"

This is the first step in finding common ground and experiencing some unity. The step to the next agenda item will be easier.

Determining What You Want to Be (5 min.)

If everyone has not read the Introduction of *Pastor Search Committee Primer* entitled "What Shall We Call Our Committee?" stop and do this now.

Hold a brief discussion to find if there is consensus on this matter; and if there is, make it a matter of record. The benefits of this will become more obvious as you progress through your task.

Ascertaining the Steps to Be Followed (10 min.)

At the end of this chapter is a list of possible objectives for the committee to use. Take time now to do the following:

1. Determine if anyone has a question concerning the meaning of any of them. Clarify if needed.

2. Check to see if there is objection to the intention (not just wording) of any. If so, resolve the problem if possible.

3. Decide if any words need to be adjusted to fit your particular situation.

4. Verify these (as amended) as the objectives your committee will use to complete your endeavor.

Reminder: Those who have read the *Primer* will understand that these objectives are guideposts for your pursuit as a committee.

Discovering How Closely Your Thinking Relates to the Others of the Committee (60-90 min.)

"Reverend Grieve was a fine man, and I'm sure he did our church a lot of good; but I feel we all agree we need a different kind of person to be our next pastor," was the way Mr. Fish began the discussion about what type of pastor the committee thought they needed.

While Mr. Fish had to be at least partially correct in his terse assessment, he had really said nothing with which the others could compare their deepest feelings, much less the facts of the situation.

It is extremely difficult for members of a Pastor Search Committee to disclose their personal stance unless everyone is dealing with the same facts under the same rules of discussion. The materials at the end of this chapter entitled "An Exercise for a Pastor Search Committee to Find Consensus About a Pastor's Time Priorities" should allow you to stay within this framework.

You will find a set of cards on which is printed twelve roles in which pastors find themselves. None of these is wrong or bad. Your responsibility is to assess your church's priorities of the time available to the person you call as pastor.

Several factors should or could color your thinking. Will the position be full-time? (Are you going to allow educational pursuits or other vocational opportunities?) Is there some unusual factor about your congregation that has a dramatic effect upon available time regardless of your desires? (The extremes would be a rural church on the plains of Kansas where miles and miles are required for even the basic ministries or an inner-city church in Atlanta where crisis situations can overwhelm the best-laid plans.)

Finally, be sure to consider the uniqueness of your congregation and community even though it may not be dramatically unusual. (The age of your church, the sociological factors of the bulk of the congregation, and the type of community in which the church is located are matters for consideration.)

After reflecting on these factors and then making sure that everyone understands the process, you should then go through the exercise.

When the time comes for revealing how the priorities were rated, there must be complete freedom of expression. Though a member's stance on a priority may prove to be different from the consensus (and this will happen to almost everyone), this will be valuable knowledge for the others as the operation of the committee continues in the future.

Praying for Leadership (15 min.)

There is always the need for prayer, and this is particularly true for a Pastor Search Committee. However, hopefully you can develop the desire to engage in prayer that is specific. It would seem legitimate to take into consideration the situation of the moment in your journey in searching for a pastor.

At this stage of your work you are concerned about relationships. The committee has a real need to develop a bond of love. Pray that this will occur. You have also begun to explore insights. Pray for the Lord to give you insight into the desires of the congregation, the best way to do your work, and the motive for the recommendations you will be receiving.

Assignments

Read all of them, before making any—thus avoiding misusing someone.

Task 1: Electing officers of committee

If the group has chosen to wait until this time, elect a committee chairperson and other appropriate officers. Write in on front inside cover.

Task 2: The Commissioning Service

1. Choose a person to talk to the interim pastor or person in charge about using this service next Sunday.

Person Chosen_____

2. Select an individual to contact music director and deacon chairman concerning their roles in the service.

Person Chosen_____

3. Decide on testimony subjects.
   a. Topic:_____Person_____
   b. Topic:_____Person_____
   c. Topic:_____Person_____

4. Name a member to briefly explain to the congregation this event in the service prior to the commissioning.

Person Named_____

Task 3: Congregational Survey

1. Appoint a person to work with those in charge of developing the morning worship format to include time for the questionnaire.

Person Appointed_____

2. Determine who will acquire copies of questionnaire if the number in the kit is not sufficient for your congregation.

Person Determined_____

3. Appoint a subcommittee to tabulate the survey results before next committee meeting. Evaluation of results by this subcommittee is optional.

_____
_____
_____

Task 4: A Report to the Congregation

Though several of the tasks outlined require reports, there should be general information reports week by week. After this first session, the chairman should report; then the other committee members follow in subsequent sessions.

Possible Objectives

1. Reach general agreement as to the committee task; then set basic ground rules to follow.

2. Structure a systematic approach for screening recommendations.

3. Devise a plan of communication with the congregation which includes sharing how the committee will function and when reports are to be expected.

4. Formulate the procedures for conducting interviews with prospective pastor.

5. Research, organize, and outline for presentation the necessary information about the church which will be of value to possible pastors.

6. Devise an appropriate overview of the community served by the church, and show how the church relates to the community.

7. Agree upon the guidelines that will be used in making the transition from a positive, responsive interview to a possible call.

8. Develop a carefully arranged presentation of the prospective pastor to the congregation.

9. Reach agreement about what is involved in the termination of the work of the committee.

An Exercise for a Pastor Search Committee to Find Consensus About a Pastor's Time Priorities

Read through the entire stack of cards that list the priorities of time for a pastor. After you have done this, place the card describing the "most important" priority in column 1. From the remaining eleven cards, select the "least important" priority and put that card in column 5. From the remaining ten cards, select three "more important" and put those cards in column 2. From the remaining seven, select three "less important" and put those cards in column 4. Put the last four cards in the center column (column 3). This is actually done on a tabletop as in the chart below. Placement in the chart determines point values.

Col. 1	Col. 2	Col. 3	Col. 4	Col. 5
☐	☐	☐	☐	☐
	☐	☐	☐	
	☐	☐	☐	
		☐		

5 pts. each   4 pts. each   3 pts. each   2 pts. each   1 pt. each

Note: If fewer than seven people are using this exercise, change point values to 10, 8, 6, 4, and 2.)

After each person on the committee has done this, each tells how he has rated each priority (Enabler, Visitor, etc.) beginning with column 1. That point total is transferred to the column under his name on the reverse of this sheet.

Personal Skills Developer
(1 Tim. 4:15)

In today's world, a person must be a lifelong learner. This is especially true for a minister since he must be using his skills almost daily with a congregation which constantly needs to be challenged. Continuing education opportunities are expanding and should be used regularly.

Administrator
(Titus 1:8*b*)

The key to understanding this term is to remember that it comes from the same root word as *minister*. To be an administrator in a church is to see that the people are organized and challenged to be involved in ministry both within and outside the congregation.

Leader
(Titus 2:7-8)

There are times when a pastor has to use skills that are not easily defined. He must be able to get groups within the church or the congregation as a whole to follow him on certain issues or to meet certain church needs. He has to work at developing these skills and at gaining their acceptance.

Family Provider
(1 Tim. 3:4-5; 5:8)

It is easy to see this as outside the time priority of a pastor. Many have an attitude that this will be done apart from the congregation's encouragement. This is true to a point; but shouldn't the congregation say pointedly, "We want you to spend time with your family"?

Teacher
(1 Tim. 4:11-13)

For the pastor, the teacher/preacher roles are often so interchangeable as to seem to be only one. However, there are times when teaching needs to be done. Doctrine is better learned from teaching tools than preaching. Principles may be absorbed more quickly if taught rather than imparted through traditional preaching methods.

Proclaimer
(2 Tim. 4:2)

A pastor must develop from fifty to one hundred sermons or messages a year. For this task to be possible, much less be well done, requires a lot of preparation in the way of continuous wide study. The very act of delivering these messages in a persuasive manner also requires expending considerable energy which must be replenished.

Counselor
(2 Tim. 3:16-17)

Every church has troubled people. A pastor must meet their needs as far as his skills and time will allow him. Knowledge of how to do effective referring is also a part of a pastor's counselor role.

Evangelizer
(Titus 1:9)

This is not to be confused with the preaching pastor/evangelist. The reference is to the time given by a pastor in working outside the church membership. This includes reaching unchurched Christians and sharing the gospel with people who have not had a personal relationship with Jesus Christ.

Community Supporter
(1 Tim. 3:7)

When moral issues arise in a community, the pastor who has served in some civic capacity or participated in other community events will be more likely to be listened to than someone who has remained withdrawn from the community.

Enabler
(2 Tim. 2:2)

Some people (even leaders) never develop their skills and gifts if they are used only within large groups. Personal attention must be given from time to time. At the very least, there must be training within small groups.

Visitor
(1 Tim. 3:2)

In contrast to the evangelizer role, the visitor role is primarily within the church membership. It includes hospital, shut-in, and bereavement visits. It also takes in ministering to families who are having internal problems. However, it should as far as possible entail visiting church members just for the purpose of becoming better acquainted.

Denominational Supporter
(1 Tim. 4:16)

Denominations which have congregational government must of necessity depend upon the *voluntary* efforts of pastors and church leaders to carry out their cooperative efforts. These may be on several different denominational levels.

Using the Congregational Questionnaires

If you will take time to assure the people of the church that this is an opportunity to express themselves about some characteristics of the future pastor, they will respond and fill out the questionnaire.

However, you must take a further step. Give them a specific time to answer the questions and directions for how to do it. In most congregations, a Sunday morning service is best. Normally the largest concentration of people occurs in the worship service.

With good preparation, the whole matter can be accomplished in fifteen minutes. Follow these steps:

1. Get the official approval of the church, if necessary.

2. Alert the person who plans the service of the need of a fifteen-minute segment.

3. Have the questionnaires ready for quick distribution by the ushers (also pencils, if necessary).

4. Have a person prepared to give brief instructions; read the questions as the people answer them. (Instructions should simply be to check the blank which seems immediately correct. Caution should be given against using "not

sure'' more than once or twice.)

5. Have everyone pass them to the aisle to their right for collection by the ushers.

Depending upon when the Pastor Search Committee will next meet, have a subcommittee tally the results that afternoon or in the near future.

The Commissioning Service

To be effective, this service must be used before the Pastor Search Committee becomes highly visible in its work. The ideal time is the second Sunday after the election of the committee.

There is a packet of outlines of the commissioning service in the resource kit. These are for use by all the people who will be participating. This may be reproduced (in personalized form) in the regular bulletin on the Sunday it is to be used.

Hymn themes have been suggested rather than specific hymns because of the great varieties of hymnals. This is also true of the responsive reading.

The verses listed below are most helpful if a modern Bible translation is used. You may want to use different passages.

Further help in the planning for and the importance of this service will be found by listening to the cassette tape in the resource kit.

Passages from Paul
Philippians 2:1 ff.
'Philippians 2:14-15
1 Timothy 3:1-7
1 Timothy 5:17 ff.
1 Timothy 2:15
2 Timothy 1:14
2 Timothy 3:14-17
2 Timothy 4:2
Titus 1:6 ff.

Titus 1:15
Titus 2:7-8
Titus 3:9a
Proverbs 8:12
Proverbs 9:10
Proverbs 11:15
Proverbs 12:4
Proverbs 12:25
Proverbs 14:26
Proverbs 15:15-16
Proverbs 15:22-23
Proverbs 15:31-32
Proverbs 16:9
Proverbs 18:12-13
Proverbs 18:15
Proverbs 18:17
Proverbs 20:5
Proverbs 20:24
Proverbs 23:12
Proverbs 24:3-4
Proverbs 24:26
Proverbs 25:12
Proverbs 26:22
Proverbs 27:1-2
Proverbs 27:9
Proverbs 27:19
Proverbs 29:2

Study Session 2—Structuring a Systematic Approach for Screening Prospective Pastors

Agenda:
    Reasoning out the need
    Thinking through the process
    Deciding upon the proper materials
    Assigning undergirds good results
    Concluding with intercession
Objectives:
    At the conclusion of this session—
    1. You will be able to explain to anyone who raises the question *why* the committee chose this approach for screening.
    2. You will have analyzed the materi-

als and forms to the extent that you can feel comfortable in personalizing them for use by your Pastor Search Committee.

3. You will have begun to feel the burden of the spiritual responsibility that a person takes on when one chooses to recommend a pastor for a church.

Reasoning Out the Need (5 min.)

Much of what was done by "pulpit committees" in the past was pure (or in many cases quite impure) tradition. Nowhere was this more true than in the matter of screening prospects. It was usually a matter of going to hear someone preach from a pulpit. Usually, but not always, this person had been recommended as someone who might make the church a good preacher.

If you have really worked to this point in this book, you are already committed to more than that. But here are a few more ideas that will enable you to see the value of this approach.

You will want to use a process that is fair to everyone. This one is patently fair. You are trying to gain much information about each person recommended. This method assists you in that quest. You intend to maintain order and avoid discord in the midst of the process. This plan gives you that assurance. You are set on being open with the possible candidates as you advance in your relationship with them. This arrangement gives you that privilege. You are committed to having profitable interviews. This strategy promises you that opportunity.

Thinking Through the Process (25 min.)

Step 1: Only prospects with written recommendations in committee files will be considered. This applies to recom-

mendations from church members as well as from people outside the church.

Step 2: Only prospects whose references have been checked will be considered.

Step 3: At each meeting of the committee, prospects meeting standards of Steps 1 and 2 will be given priority ranking. The committee will decide whether it will deal with more than one prospect at a time during this stage.

Step 4: When a prospect becomes a top priority candidate, he will be personally contacted by the committee chairman to determine his interest and availability.

Step 5: If the person is interested, a date will be agreed upon for the committee to hear the candidate and to have an extended interview.

These five steps are discussed in detail in the *Primer*. If some have not recently read the discussion, take the time to review this information for the whole group.

Following the general discussion, the committee will deal with the steps one by one, either adopting or rejecting. If by chance any are rejected, another idea which will fit into the process must be chosen in order for continuity to be maintained.

Deciding Upon the Proper Materials (30 min.)

At the end of this chapter, you will find an assortment of forms. These are planned and correlated for use with the screening procedures suggested previously. Following is a brief overview of each form with attention given to key features.

Item: Personal Recommendation Information

This form is mailed (or given) along

with an explanatory letter to every person intending to make a recommendation. This is true even when the person has made a recommendation in another manner.

• Key Feature: A person who cannot give an adequate answer to the question "Why do you feel this person would be a good pastor for this church?" probably has a weak recommendation.

Item: Sample Letter to Person Making a Recommendation

This is not the basic explanatory letter, but the letter sent when forms are sent to someone who has used another means of making an unsolicited recommendation.

• Key Feature: Reasoning is given for repetition, thus overcoming objections to extra effort.

Item: Sample Letter for Checking a Reference

To give basic ingredients for a letter that will elicit a reply is the purpose of this letter. You will use your own terminology, but be sure you include all the ideas emphasized.

• Key Feature: Your enclosure, which is information to help reference write a better evaluation of the prospect.

Item: Character Reference Inquiry

This is the enclosure with the letter to the reference. Its purpose is to ensure a reply. Even persons who will not write a letter will ordinarily fill out a questionnaire.

• Key Feature: The ratings on personal characteristics. These should be studied for clues which might lead to further inquiry.

Item: Personal Data Information

The difference between this and the first item is that the first tells what someone thinks he knows about an individual, while in this one the prospect shares personal information. Since it is person-al, the questions are more direct on some matters. Two other advantages of using this form are the opportunity to compare information and additional references to check.

• Key Feature: The question regarding the candidate's current status. This answer warrants special study.

To make your job easier, compositions are printed in the typed form. You can find a typewriter which will match and fill in the blanks which will personalize the material. Permission is granted to duplicate these forms for use by your committee. Directions are copyrighted and may not be copied in any manner.

Assignments (Read All Before Delegating Any)

Task 1: Designate a committee member to share with the congregation during regular services over a period of several weeks what the process will be for screening recommendations.

Person delegated_____

Task 2: Place the responsibility for condensing the material you have studied into prime data which can be printed in the church bulletins and newsletters. (See chapter on communications.)

Person responsible_____

Task 3: Deputize a member of your group to have all needed material reproduced. Send word to the church staff (or association office or print shop) that this person will have this responsibility during the term of the committee.

Person deputized_____

Task 4: Commission someone (if appropriate, the chairman) to develop the letters to be used. These should not be reproduced but are to be typed personally. A person with utmost integrity should do the typing if a committee member does not have this capability.

Person commissioned_____

Task 5: Enlist a member of your group to keep a current list of people who have become involved in helping you (recommenders, references, interim pastor, office staff, etc.). Have this list ready for sharing at prayer time each meeting.

Person enlisted_____

Concluding with Intercession (15 min.)

As your committee comes to this stage in its work, the journey begins to get personal. That is, you are going to begin to be in contact with and develop some dependence upon a lot of people. You want them to respond to your requests in as personal a manner as possible. Suggestions have been made about how to draw out their best, but one thing is needed.

These people need to go on your prayer lists. It is a prodigal act on your part to seek their special assistance or cooperation and not provide for them your prayerful intercession. This should be done at your regular committee sessions as well as in private devotions.

Retreat Agenda for Pastor Search Committee

This is a new concept, but one which should be given utmost consideration for three reasons outlined in chapter 1 of the *Primer.*

The retreat outlined will be for a Friday night—Saturday approach, but it can easily be adapted to fit your schedule. However, it will only work if it can be arranged to be the "kick-off" plan for the committee's work.

Friday Night

7:00 PM Chapter 1: Study Session 1—Building a Plan for Action

9:00 PM Chapter 1: Study Session 2—Structuring a Systematic Approach

Breaks will be determined partially by committee size. A small committee (five persons) can finish session 1 in under two hours. Larger committees should plan "stand-up" breaks and have refreshments available all the time rather than at a specific break.

Saturday Morning

8:30 AM Chapter 2: Study Session—Learning to Recognize the Signs

Ask one member to give a fifteen-minute review of chapter 6 of the *Primer.* Ask another for a ten-minute review of the first four sections of this study session. Spend the balance of the hour in group discussion of the "Plan of Communication."

9:30—10:00 Break

10:00 AM Chapter 3: Study Session— Taking Stock of the Present Situation

11:00 AM Review Development Sessions in Chapters 1—3

You will notice that all previous retreat time has been spent on study sessions. There has to be a time gap between study and development sessions for preparation of materials and gathering of information. However, if the committee will do an overview of these development sessions, it will be excellent preparation and offer a good picture of the total committee responsibility for the coming weeks.

Saturday Afternoon

Noon—Lunch 1:00 PM Alternative Activities

Highly experienced committees may want to move on to chapter 1 development session. There is a danger of rushing the natural progress of the methodology; thus this should be done with utmost caution.

Most committees are going to need this time for catching up on the proposed schedule. It will vary from committee to committee, but inevitably a group will feel justified in abandoning the schedule to spend more time on one of the development activities.

3:00 PM Adjourn

Reminder: The cassette tape "Keep On Talking" should be a resource used at various times during the retreat. An advanced listening session by the chairman will make it easy to determine the appropriate segments to be used as well as the proper timing.

Development Session 1—Moving from Study to Practice

Agenda:
Review the actions of study sessions. Are you satisfied?
Take the time for a period of prayer.
Start the process of screening prospects.
Give necessary assignments.

Objectives:
As a result of this session—

1. You will have analyzed the congregational survey and compared it to the consensus of your committee "priority exercise" to verify compatibility of thinking.

2. You will have checked assignments from study session 2 and accepted them or made suggestions for change.

3. You will have sorted all recommendations into three categories.

4. You will have begun to pray about the first group of possible pastoral candidates.

Reviewing Previous Actions (30 min.)

Without a doubt by this time you have experienced some sleep disturbances as well as unexpected lack of concentration in your daily responsibilities. All this means is that you have taken seriously the work of the first two study sessions. Now that a bit of time has passed, you need to check your feelings about what has occurred.

Perhaps the best way to do this is to raise a few questions for brief discussion.

1. Are you beginning to feel a sense of group commitment as well as personal commitment?

2. Is anyone having problems with the methodology used to this point? If so, will patience prevail?

3. Was adequate time given for assignments to be done in a first-class manner and by the date truly needed?

4. Does your committee feel that it is in step with the congregation; and can you already sense their spiritual rapport?

As you struggle with these questions you will find that they are leading you over possible obstacles that would pop up if the questions were not considered.

Preparing for Ignition (15 min.)

Anxiety is your foe. It is understandable to be anxious to get on with the discussion of prospects who have been recommended to you. But there is the need to pause for prayer. Before a spaceship is launched, there is utmost attention given to being ready for ignition. The engines of the rockets are not started and *then* preparation made for blast-off; all this is done in advance.

All of those procedures of the study sessions and the activities done in this session are a part of that preparation. The most important thing to do now is to stop and pray. This is not a time for rote prayers, sentence prayers, or casual prayers.

This is the occasion for setting aside sufficient time to invoke God's participation in the awesome task that is yours.

You are concerned with the future of your church. The ministries of God-called people can be at stake. You have one overriding objective—to search out God's choice for your church.

You are going to have to be open to God's will and to be concerned that others will also know that will.

If there are members of your committee who cannot participate in open prayer, be sure to give time for private prayer. Though personal needs and requests cannot be ignored, keep at the heart of your supplications the power of God and the leadership of the Holy Spirit in the total effort in which you are involved.

Getting the Process Under Way (30 min.)

The first step in the screening procedures is that all recommendations must be in written form. Adhering to this principle means that you can divide all recommendations received so far into three categories.

The largest category in all probability is written recommendations which do not meet the criterion of your committee. There will require a two-step procedure. First, the recommendation as received is examined to see if the person has the basic qualifications for consideration. (If in doubt, give consideration.) When this is positive, step 2 will be to send a letter of explanation and appropriate forms to the person making the recommendations. The committee may wish to delegate the responsibility for step 1 to the committee chairperson. This will often save time in getting the required types of recommendations in the hands of the committee.

The second kind of recommendation is the oral one. If the person(s) these were given to has not already followed through, then the recommenders should be contacted with instructions and forms for acceptable recommendations.

The third type of recommendation is composed of those in written form which include all the information your committee has required. Ordinarily, these will be from people who asked for the privilege of making a recommendation or who sent an incorrect one earlier but who have already responded to your request. These are the only ones with which you are ready to concern yourselves.

Your first consideration with the prospects who have qualified through step 1 of the screening process is to contact their references. If you lack enthusiasm for this, you may want to review the section in chapter 2 of the *Primer*. You will not want to delay getting this under way, however.

The necessary resources are included in the materials at the end of this chapter.

Assignments (10 min.)

Task 1: Check to see who needs more time for completing the study sessions. Evaluate whether this precludes additional tasks at this time.

Task 2: Agree upon the chairperson or choose another member to coordinate the requests for correct recommendations. Person Chosen_____

Task 3: Settle upon the committee member best suited to contact the references. Member_____

Development Session 2—Continuing the Determination of Prime Prospects

Agenda:

Receive all new information on prospects

Distribute appropriate materials
Evaluate the qualified candidates
Begin the contact process
Respond to prayer concerns
Continue tasks already assigned

Objectives:

As an achievement of this session—

1. You will have expanded your usable data on prospective pastors.

2. You will be encouraged by the quality of prospects.

3. You will have begun to assume a spiritual concern for ministers you have not met.

Note: This particular development session is one which should be adjusted to fit the schedule of each committee. Some committees will take up some agenda items in the first development session. *Most committees will repeat this session several times.*

Reception of New Information
(10-30 min.)

How many times have you experienced a situation in which a heavy discussion was broken by "Oh, I forgot to give you some information I got in the mail this week"? If such an experience is not disruptive, it is at least disconcerting.

To avoid this, you should provide for the input of new information at the beginning of each session. There will be vast amounts of fresh material in the early development sessions. It will fall into two classifications and should be dealt with separately and in order.

First, new recommendations will be heard. If these have been properly done, the information should have been reproduced for distribution.

Recommendations which do not meet committee criteria will simply be announced as received and disposition made which the committee had previously agreed upon as policy.

The second classification of new information is that of reference responses. This should be in reproduced form and with sufficient copies for all committee members. It will be shared after the group has been brought up to date on all new recommendations.

Distribution of Appropriate Materials
(10-30 min.)

It is important how and when you distribute the additional information gathered since you last met. Committee members need to be able to absorb as much data as possible on each individual before they begin to compare the data. This is especially true of the basic information found in the recommendation. If the committee members do not study and truly learn the basics about each person, then they are going to be constantly confused when discussions about strengths and weaknesses begin. One way to ensure this is to distribute material about only one prospect at a time. After all members have studied it, pass out information on the next candidate. Naturally, each member of the committee will want to pursue this on his own time between sessions.

It logically follows that reference responses should be handled in like manner. Of course, you will have multiple responses about the same person; so these should be grouped accordingly before being apportioned.

Evaluation of Qualified Candidates
(30-60 min.)

When a person gets through the previous steps, he has at least the basic qualifications for consideration as God's choice for your church. However, even though you are working with the basics, you have learned enough to be able to begin giving priority ranking to the candidates who have qualified to this point.

Some committees will feel that they have had sufficient discussion during the previous steps to move right into the ranking process. Others may want to have brief summary-type discussions before starting to rank. Keep in mind that the discussions may serve an additional purpose. If the discussion is generally negative about a prospect (especially after responses from references), then he is eliminated from consideration prior to ranking.

The purpose of ranking is to set priorities for which candidates will be contacted and in what order. It is a never-ending process as long as recommendations are received and until serious negotiations begin with a specific person.

Ranking can be done informally as long as no more than five people are under consideration. When you have more than five at one session, you should have each member rank the top five individually. Number 1 is given five points, number 2 four points, number 3 three points, etc. After all members have done this, the totals determine the top five. All others are removed from consideration unless additional information is received which warrants reevaluation.

New candidates are prioritized in the same manner, having to move into standing by the same process with the current top five. This gives a person recommended two months into your committee tenure the same opportunity a person has who was recommended the second week.

You are now ready to contact the person with the top priority ranking. Once you make this contact and he indicates a willingness to proceed with steps of consideration, this prospect remains number 1 until he is eliminated after the interview or another step of the process. (There is an alternate plan used by some committees discussed in the *Primer*.)

In some cases, after you have ranked your prospects the first time, you may choose to wait a reasonable time before pursuing the number 1 prospect. This should certainly be done if there is a lack of notable enthusiasm, though this will be rare when you have followed correct methodology designed to draw strong recommendations.

Manifestation of Interest in a Candidate

The most effective way to show your interest in a prospect is to simply tell him you are interested. He is probably aware of it, perhaps by the forms you sent him (see Personal Data Information) or by word from a reference. The question in his mind is, "How interested are you?"

You will find ample reason in the *Primer* for going ahead with a personal contact, so let's cover a few of the details the chairperson is usually responsible for carrying out.

First, be aware that the prospect has the same right as the Pastor Search Committee to terminate a relationship between the two of you at any point. You cannot assume his interest. When you call, you begin by sharing the feelings of your committee and then immediately inquire as to whether the feeling is mutual. If the answer is *no*—and it will be sometimes—you go back to the committee unless they have given prior permission to move to the next person on the list. Then the same procedure is followed.

When the response is positive, a date

is agreed upon for hearing the candidate preach and having an interview session.

You will want to avoid holidays and special occasions in either church. Also, you will want to allow adequate time for the work the committee must accomplish before it is ready for an interview.

Continuation of Tasks Already Begun (5-15 min.)

Often the committee can take a break in its session while the chairperson telephones the prospect. When this is done, it keeps the whole committee informed and simplifies further assignments. Otherwise:

Task 1: The chairperson is to notify all committee members of the response and the date which has been set for hearing and interviewing.

Task 2: Check on previous assignments and give help as needed for continuation.

Perception of Prayer Needs (15 min.)

The Pastor Search Committee has an awareness of all the people involved in their efforts. This is beyond comprehension by any other person or groups of persons at this time.

This gives you the spiritual privilege of expressing thanksgiving for their help and of interceding on their behalf as they seek to aid you. In this period of concern, pray for them by name.

Scale for Determining Priorities of
Minister's Time

PRIORITIES	Name 1	2	3	4	5	6	7	Total
Personal Skills Developer								
Family Provider								
Administrator								
Teacher								
Leader								
Proclaimer								
Counselor								
Enabler								
Evangelizer								
Visitor								
Community Supporter								
Denominational Supporter								

After each person on the committee has "valued" all of the priorities, add the columns to the right to get the cumulative value which the committee has placed on each priority.

What Do I Expect of My Pastor?

Strongly Agree	Agree	Not Sure	Disagree	Strongly Disagree	

PROCLAMATION MINISTRY

Strongly Agree	Agree	Not Sure	Disagree	Strongly Disagree	
___	___	___	✓	___	1. I don't think it is necessary to give an invitation at the conclusion of each worship service.
✓	___	___	___	___	2. I do want at least 50% of the sermons which my pastor preaches to be aimed specifically at providing Christian growth.
✓	___	___	___	___	3. I do not think it is important that my pastor spend at least 10 hours each week on sermon preparation.
___	___	___	___	___	4. I do not see any connection between my pastor's personal visitation program and the kinds of sermons he preaches.

FELLOWSHIP MINISTRY

___	___	___	___	___	1. I see a very valid use of the worship service as a means of increasing fellowship within the congregation.
___	___	___	___	___	2. I do not think my pastor need be capable of relating in a personal way with all age groups in the church.
___	___	___	___	___	3. I believe my pastor should use the present fellowship strengths of the church to emphasize outreach possibilities.
___	___	___	___	___	4. I do not think it matters whether my pastor understands how the educational programs of the church can be used as instruments of fellowship.

LEADERSHIP MINISTRY

___	___	___	___	___	1. I expect my pastor to be able to give guidance to staff personnel in such a manner as to ensure harmonious programs in the church.
___	___	___	___	___	2. I believe there is little value in the pastor having a close relationship with the deacon body as a whole.
___	___	___	___	___	3. I am convinced that my pastor must work closely with the organizational leaders in order to experience church growth.
___	___	___	___	___	4. I want my pastor to engage in continuing education opportunities so he can continue to develop his leadership skills.

HELPING MINISTRY

___	___	___	___	___	1. I do not think it is necessary for my pastor to give a large portion of his time for hospital and shut-in visitation.
___	___	___	___	___	2. I would agree that "troubled people" can dominate my pastor's time unless he places limitations on himself.
___	___	___	___	___	3. I would prefer that my pastor learn what community helps are available for people and make use of them when this would not conflict with Christian convictions.
___	___	___	___	___	4. I believe it is a waste of time for my pastor to work to develop the laity to become ministers to one another.

ORGANIZATIONAL MINISTRY

___	___	___	___	___	1. I believe the Sunday School is the "church growth" arm of the church and my pastor should give it his strong support.
___	___	___	___	___	2. I see the music program of the church as being a ministry in which my pastor should not interfere.
___	___	___	___	___	3. I would like for my pastor to leave the mission opportunities of the church primarily to the women.
___	___	___	___	___	4. I think giving guidance to developing training opportunities for all church members would be too frustrating to be worth my pastor's time.

PERSONAL RECOMMENDATION INFORMATION

(Please try to answer all questions; use back of
sheets as necessary)

DATE_____

NAME_____AGE_____

PRESENT ADDRESS_____
                    Street or Box   City   State   Zip Code

_____
                    Phone Number

PRESENT POSITION_____

     Length of Service_____Years _____Months

PREVIOUS PAID CHURCH-RELATED EXPERIENCE (Please list positions, length of service, size of church, and *reason for leaving* last three positions. Last position first, etc.):

OTHER EXPERIENCE PERSON HAS HAD WHICH WOULD BE HELPFUL TO A COMMITTEE:

EDUCATION (From highest back: school name, degree, date):

FAMILY INFORMATION

Spouse's Name and Age_____

Please write a brief paragraph concerning your mate's strengths in Christian service:

Names and ages of children:

REFERENCES:

Name, Address, and Phone of One Professor_____

_____

Name, Address, and Phone of One Pastor_____

_____

Name, Address, and Phone of One Church Member from previous place of service_____

_____

There must be three references; please substitute if you do not know the categories of people requested above.

Person making this recommendation_____

Why do you feel this person would be a good pastor for this church? (This must be answered.)

SAMPLE LETTER REQUESTING A FORMAL RECOMMENDATION

Dr. John Knox
Highland Church
Glascow, GA 77777

Dear Dr. Knox:

Thank you for your recent letter of recommendation regarding Rev. Frank Campbell. Your gracious concern for the needs of our church and the work of our committee is appreciated.

Because we are seeking to follow a specific plan in our task as a Pastor Search Committee, we would like one further favor from you. We use a standardized form for recommendations; and, though it asks for repetitious material, would you please fill it out completely and return in the enclosed envelope?

Again, let us acknowledge our gratitude to you for what you have done and ask that you remember to continue to pray for us.

Sincerely,

SAMPLE LETTER FOR CHECKING A REFERENCE

Mr. Good N. Spirit
1421 King's Highway
Bestyet, Texas 00666

Dear Mr. Spirit:

The Pastor Search Committee of the Ideal Baptist Church has been given your name as a reference for _____.

Our committee is very interested in your evaluation of _____ and will be awaiting your reply before proceeding with our consideration of him. You would honor us and greatly assist us if you would give us a forthright and honest opinion of this person. We will honor and respect you by being discreet with the information.

To help you in your evaluation, we are enclosing some information about our church and community. We are also sending a brief form for you to fill out.

However, we would greatly appreciate a narrative evaluation which might include your perception of: his pastoral skills, preaching ability, personal relationships, accomplishments in ministry and any other positive or negative factors you feel would be valuable to us. You do not have to be formal; just turn this page over and use the back side.

Thank you for taking the time to share with us in this time of need. Please pray for our committee as we seek God's choice for our church.

Sincerely,

Enclosures (2)

NAME OF PROSPECT_____AGE_____

CHARACTER REFERENCE INQUIRY

The person whose name appears above has been recommended to us. Please give us information requested below and any additional comment. Information will be kept confidential.

1. How long have you known the prospect?_____
2. Are you a friend of the family?_____
3. How does he spend his time? (hobbies, etc.)_____
_____

4. Please rate the prospect:
We aren't looking for a perfect person, so be straightforward.

Qualifications	Excellent	Good	Fair	Poor	Very Poor	?
Character						
Conduct						
Work Attitude						
Ability to Get Along with Others						
Cooperation						
Dependability						
Honesty						
Personal Habits						
Emotional Maturity						

5. Additional comments:

_____
    Signed   Date

Please return to _____ Church

Address_____

PERSONAL DATA INFORMATION FOR _____ CHURCH

DATE_____

NAME_____AGE_____

PRESENT ADDRESS_____
Street or Box   City   State   Zip

_____
Phone Number

PRESENT POSITION_____
Length of service: _____Years _____months

PREVIOUS PAID CHURCH-RELATED EXPERIENCE (Please list positions, length of service, size of church, and reason you left last three positions. Last position first, etc.):

Are you happy in your present position?_____Write on back of this sheet why you answered as you did.

OTHER EXPERIENCE YOU HAVE HAD WHICH WOULD BE HELPFUL TO A CHURCH COMMITTEE:

EDUCATION (From highest back—school name, degree, date):

WHAT TYPE OF FINANCIAL ARRANGEMENT IS NECESSARY TO MEET THE PRESENT NEEDS OF YOUR FAMILY? (We realize you are not able to be absolute; we only want to see if we are compatible at these points.)

If Full-Time:
    Base Salary $_____per month
    Housing $_____per month, if no parsonage
    Car Allowance $_____per month
    Annuity Programs $_____per month
    Convention Allowance $_____per year
    Other $_____

IF A STUDENT, PLEASE GIVE PLANNED GRADUATION DATE: _____, 19____
(Explain any contingencies.)

FAMILY INFORMATION:

Spouse—Name and Age:_____

Please write a brief paragraph concerning her strengths in Christian service:

Will she do secular work?_____If so, what type and explain briefly skills involved:

Names and ages of children:

REFERENCES:

Name, Address, and Phone of One Professor_____

_____

Name, Address, and Phone of One Pastor_____

_____

Name, Address, and Phone of One Church Member from some previous place of service

_____

NOTE: You may substitute Association Director of Missions for one of the above_____

_____

2

Touching All Bases

Study Session—Learning to Recognize the Signs

Agenda:
Taking advantage of open doors
Disciplining yourselves to be consistent
Strengthening the trust level
Engaging in mutual prayer support
Identifying tasks for assignments

Objectives:
When you finish this session—

1. You will be challenged to enlarge the congregation's view of the responsibilities of the Pastor Search Committee.

2. You will be ready to take steps to set up regular communication channels with the congregation.

3. You will be aware of new spiritual opportunities which are yours because of your participation in the Pastor Search Committee.

Taking Advantage of Open Doors
(5 min.)

One of the basic mistakes made by many Pastor Search Committees is to look for ways to guarantee secrecy in its work rather than concentrating on developing awareness of the resources available. There are matters which do need to be confidential, but in many cases there is information which should be shared.

When you begin, you will find that al-most everyone you should have a relationship with during the course of your work will be open to you and anxious to assist. If you fail to use these open doors, you may very well find them shut later when you feel the need to use them.

Openness in communication should begin early in your efforts. You have four target groups you will communicate with at various stages. The first is the body who elected you. Even as they put their trust in you in electing you, you need to immediately let them know how important you feel that continued trust really is. The key to keeping that door unlocked is the Commissioning Service.

The next target group might be termed outside helpers. This group would include people who make recommendations and those who respond as references. Your primary responsibility to them is to make sure they understand what methodology you are using, why you want certain information, and how important their help is.

Another group which stands ready to help you are individual church members. This will not be a large group; yet you will always find some people ready to take special assignments without insisting on being on the inside about confidential matters. Each committee will become aware of both the need and the persons in its own way.

The last classification of persons who

need to be communicated with effectively by your committee is the hold-over staff of your church. This may range from a part-time secretary to a professional staff of ten or fifteen people. You will find them a valuable resource if you let them know you want them to be.

Disciplining Yourselves to Be Consistent (3 min.)

When one church member hears from another church member special information about your work which has not been made public, your task has become at least one degree more difficult. The person who hears wonders why he wasn't included in hearing the same information. After all, he is a church member, too. Your goal is to share all special information in the best-attended service of your church at a time previously announced and publicized.

If you are consistent in sharing general information about your work in church services and through church publications, you can build to the special occasions such as announcing when a prospect will come before the church.

Strengthening the Trust Level (3 min.)

Being careful in these communication efforts and the others discussed in chapter 6 of the *Primer* will bring needed support to you later. Every step the Pastor Search Committee takes to gain the confidence of everyone with whom they work pays dividends when they are most needed.

Surely it makes sense that any group who feels they have been adequately informed along the way will be much more likely to respond positively when asked to make a decision.

Conversely, how can a congregation be expected to make up the knowledge gap which exists between themselves and a Pastor Search Committee who does not share information about its task but comes suddenly with a recommendation? The congregation sees a person who is not only a stranger but seemingly without credentials.

Though true trust includes responding to the unknown, the foundation has to include the proving of being worthy of trust.

Engaging in Mutual Prayer Support

The suggestion was made in chapter 1 that a person be assigned to keep a list of all people who assist your committee. This is not only done for later expressions of appreciation but to help establish your committee prayer list.

Even as you work at impressing upon all concerned your desire that they support you in prayer, you will want to give reciprocal intervention for them. Who needs your prayers more than the people who are helping you?

There is much to be said for sharing this fact that you are praying for them. It will result in a prayer partnership that will have tenure beyond the time each person is engaged in helping.

Identifying Tasks for Assignment (50 min.)

The communications tasks are spread throughout the whole process of doing the work of the Pastor Search Committee. At the end of this chapter is a section entitled "Plan of Communication." Now would be an appropriate time to take stock as to whether you are up to date on the suggestions in the plan and also to begin considering future assignments based on the plan.

Development Session—Turning Spectators into Participants

Agenda:
Calling on church members for help
Using the paid staff
Assuring that no one is overlooked
Ensuring a successful transition

Objectives:
At the completion of this session—
1. You will have determined the first group of church members who can assist your efforts in specific ways.
2. You will have determined future endeavors which will require wider participation than just the Pastor Search Committee.
3. You will have devised a plan which has the potential of communicating with every member of your church.
4. You will have started plans which will be of benefit to the eventual new pastor.

Calling on Church Members for Help

Your situation is no longer theoretical. In this session you will be making decisions about the role of people who are a part of your church fellowship.

In the chronological process you are following, you will have already discovered some needs which people outside of your committee can fill. In the case of the commissioning service, you have probably already done this.

As you begin to consider people, you should do it in the light of the total context of your work. Take an overview of all of the needs you will have and be sure to fit the people to the need that best suits their abilities.

It is assumed that you have read the *Primer* and have these needs generally in mind. This being true, a review of the "Plan of Communication" at the end of this chapter and the suggestions on "Terminating Your Work" in chapter 6 will remind you of most needs for help.

Even though the participants' involvement may be in tasks which are seemingly menial, you will want to be sure of two qualifications:
1. They must be recognized by the committee as a whole as being persons of spiritual maturity.
2. They must have the ability to keep all information they are entrusted with confidential. They are not to be the judge of its importance or timeliness. This is the prerogative of your committee. The exception would be when their responsibility is to share it as part of the communication process.

Your committee responsibilities are so great that it is a mistake to burden yourselves with responsibilities others can do. Trust yourselves to be able to make right decisions about this.

Using the Paid Staff

The first question which must be asked is, "What is each person's present status in the church?" Unless there are very strong negative responses to this question (generally speaking, not only by the committee), then the staff members deserve both respect and utilization by the Pastor Search Committee.

Some give (at least a few) staff members *ex-officio* status with the committee. This is probably not wise unless the church takes the action.

Most staff members do not want to do the work of the committee. Their desire is to be recognized as someone who can serve as a resource and then be given the privilege of exercising that ability. They also like to feel appreciated for the other extra things that fall on them when a church is pastorless.

Your committee will want to determine what its policy will be in this regard and then have a meeting with the staff person(s) involved. In this meeting you will clarify how and when you will look to them for help and at what times along the way they can expect special communication. (See especially chap. 5.)

Assuring that No One Is Overlooked

An article in the church newsletter expressed the hope that no one had been left out in the recent special church celebration. The next week there was an apology for the fact that some had indeed been overlooked. The third week there was a long list of names with further apologies offered.

This was not a Pastor Search Committee making these apologies, but the group which was making them could have avoided the problem by following some of the basic principles you should follow.

Your goal is to inform every person who is a resident member of your congregation concerning the progress of your committee in its search for God's choice for your church. That is a monumental task! You may not see it actually accomplished, but you can make it a potential reality.

Here is what you will want to do:

1. Make a list of every means of communication the church already has. This will include services and meetings where announcements can be made, newsletters, Sunday bulletins, etc.

2. Determine where the gaps are and make plans for special needs during your tenure of service. This might include extra newsletters and should involve at least two letters sent to each family of the church.

3. Agree as a committee that repetition is a valuable learning aid, and determine that you will not be deterred by some people's criticism of your reiterations of valuable information.

4. Realize that, while some people are seemingly bombarded, you are constantly seeking those who have somehow not yet gotten the message.

5. Assign responsibilities on communication if this has not been done in previous sessions.

Ensuring a Successful Transition

Someone has written about what he calls "the rites of transition." This does not advocate actual ritualistic observances. Rather, the point is made that, in the transition of responsibility (leadership), certain steps have to be taken before the process can ever be complete.

A person may never become the pastor of a group of people even though his title goes on the church sign if "the rites of transition" are never carried through.

Not many Pastor Search Committees have sensed this, though some have done it unknowingly. Your committee needs this realization now. As a part of your responsibility, you are going to help the congregation and the new pastor to have the right and meaningful relationship which every church desires and deserves.

You will find help for this in the latter stages of the *Primer* and this book, but your preparation for doing it begins now.

Plan of Communication for the Pastor Search Committee with the Congregation

1. Use a Commissioning Service (a sample is included in the Resource Kit).

2. A questionnaire may be used to get the congregation's perceptions or quali-

ties desired in a new pastor. (Sample included.)

3. Inform the congregation of basic procedures by displaying on a bulletin board forms and policy sheets which the committee is using. (See chap. 6 of the *Primer*.)

4. Print in the bulletin for several weeks the guidelines under which the committee is operating, especially regarding confidential nature of the work.

5. Place posters around the church reminding the people that the committee is at work and calling them to prayer (included in Resource Kit).

6. In at least one service each week, have a different committee member make a brief statement about the stage of the work of the committee. "We are still screening." "We will be interviewing." "We will have an announcement in approximately three weeks." Always conclude with a brief prayer period led by the person making the statement.

7. Assure the congregation that you will not make decisions for which you do not have church authority. Honor this by seeking approval through church business sessions when necessary.

8. Use bulletin inserts which are designed to prepare a church for how to get ready for a prospective pastor and how to most effectively help him begin his new work. (See the packet in the Resource Kit.)

9. Use the church newsletter to reach those not in Sunday services. Adaptations of announcements and bulletin inserts may be used.

10. Assure the congregation (and honor this) that everyone will be treated the same. No one will be informed in advance except as other committees might become involved at some stages of work.

11. Plan a Covenant Service for the first Sunday the new pastor is in the pulpit. (See the packet in the Resource Kit.)

3

Grasping the Possibilities

Study Session—Taking Stock of the Present Situation

Agenda:
Putting yourself in the shoes of the prospect
Condensing the information
Determining the time needed
Singling out the tasks to be done

Objectives:
At the conclusion of this session—

1. You will understand what kind of information about your church and community is most helpful to a prospective pastor.

2. You will have made assignments necessary to the gathering of such information.

Putting Yourself in the Shoes of the Prospect (45 min.)

Most members of the Pastor Search Committee have been members of the local church which elected them for so long that it is not easy to have an objective view about that church. It is a bit easier to honestly appraise the community served by (or, in some cases, the geographical location of) the church. But it becomes difficult again to evaluate clearly the church's place as a part of the community.

Usually this simple suggestion will help you. Try to look at your church and community as an outsider would. Particularly look at them through the eyes of a person who will be your prospective pastor.

What you are looking for is a genuine appraisal of the possibilities for your church based on the hard facts of the past and the realities of the present.

In the *Primer* and at the end of this chapter are suggestions about the kind of information which is helpful to acquire and disseminate. It will be personal because it is about your church, but it can be even more meaningful if you view it through a prospect's eyes as you write it up.

A couple of suggestions will aid you in doing this advanced step. First, do some role playing in your committee. Let each committee member assume the position of a prospect in an interview situation. Each will take a matter such as church finances, world mission support, community growth, cost of living in the community, etc., and then ask the rest of the committee probing questions. The closer the subject matter is to the member's own interest, the stronger the results will be.

Another helpful activity is to go to the next chapter on "Contacting for Response" and study the questions suggested as appropriate for interview situations.

In some cases committees will have already gathered the information. The above suggestions can be used to refine it. For other committees, these suggestions will define what needs to be sought.

Condensing the Information

It is difficult to furnish a candidate too much information about your church and community. Naturally you do not want to be redundant or to give extraneous data; but, short of those restrictions, the more the better.

It is different when sharing with persons suggested as references. They don't need to know as much. Also, if you inundate them, that may delay a response or even discourage an answer.

Your goal for sharing with references, then, is to offer them a revised standard version. It should be revised primarily through condensing it so that only facts salient to what you are asking them to do are included. Standard material may be used with every reference unless there is a justifiable reason not to do so. The version should reflect what will be most helpful to a person trying to help you assess whether a person could and should be God's choice for your church.

Determining the Time Needed

It is going to be wise for some Pastor Search Committees to stop regular meetings until all the material they deem important is gathered and put in proper form. Other committees will have the benefit of work done by some previous church group for an anniversary or other special occasion. In such situations, the task is to appropriate the information valid to the task and then update it to the present situation. Normally this can be done much more quickly.

Whatever the situation, do not get in a rush. This is another of those occasions where patience pays off in quality work and ultimately in the time needed to complete the overall task of the committee.

Singling Out the Tasks to Be Done
(15 min.)

No Pastor Search Committee is going to have readily available all of the information which portrays the possibilities of your church. What needs to be ferreted out will vary from committee to committee. Check each of the assignment suggestions to see which are applicable to your situation.

Task 1: Appoint a member to obtain a copy of the church history and to gather from it the suggested historical material.

Person appointed_____

Task 2: Delegate a member to obtain the current and recent church statistical records and to derive from them the data which the committee needs.

Person delegated_____

Task 3: Designate a member to seek some answers to the questions raised about trends in the church. These may already be known or may be raised as the information-gathering process progresses.

Person designated_____

Task 4: Commission a member to write up an analysis of the congregation which covers age-group sizes, general education level, median income level, occupations, and large interest groups. Also it may be that an estimate should be made of percentage of members with strong commitments, the leadership abilities present, etc.

Person commissioned_____

Task 5: Name a member to make a list of all the programs and ministries of the church. These might range from Mothers

Day Out to Nursing Home Ministries, or from slow pitch softball to mission tours.

Person named_____

Task 6: Appoint a segment of the committee to study the community, using the guidelines suggested in this book. Some communities can be covered by two people, but in major cities it may take three or four. Information should be sought from these sources:

1. City Government—ask for the city planning director and tell of the types of data you need.

2. Chamber of Commerce—often has more information about "people questions" and should be helpful about living standards.

3. Public school administration—besides school materials, can give insight into age-group and ethnic trends.

4. Public Library—the reference librarian will help you find census data and other statistical information.

5. Denominational offices and/or Ministerial Associations—will have readily available lists of churches.

Person(s) appointed_____
_____
_____
_____

Task 7: Deputize one member to be responsible for assimilating the materials gathered by other members. This should be done prior to the development session which is set to follow this study session.

Person deputized_____

An Overview of Our Community
I. General Characteristics
1. Classify your community: inner city, older neighborhoods, suburban, small town, rural.
2. How old is the community?
3. What are the population figures for 1965, 1970, 1975, 1980?
4. What is the average age of the adult population?
5. Characterize your community: large industry, small industry, agricultural, "bedroom" for neighboring city.

II. The People
1. Classify the majority of the people who make up the community. Be as specific as possible.
2. What are the employment characteristics? (Pay scales, local or commuter, diversified, etc.)
3. What is the mobility of the people? What is the annual percentage of families moving out of the community?
4. What is the ethnic makeup?

III. Living in this Community Usually Means . . .
1. Living in a house priced in $___ to $___ range.
2. A public school system which includes_____
_____.
3. Medical care offered through ___ hospitals, ___ doctors, ___ dentists, etc.
4. Shopping "at home" in ___shopping centers as well as the downtown area.
5. A cost of living which is above that of ___ but below ___.

IV. In Our Community Our Church Is One Among:
1. ___Southern Baptist churches
2. ___other Baptist churches
3. ___other evangelical churches
4. ___other churches in ___denominations
Check with local ministerial association if in doubt.

V. Relate the profile you get from the previous questions to your church. For instance, what are the church growth figures for 1970, 1975, and 1980? What are the employment characteristics of the congregation?

Development Session— Projecting the Purpose of Your Church

Agenda:
Reception and evaluation of material
Correlation of information
Projection of purpose

Objectives:
Upon the completion of this session—
1. You will have information about your church and community which you are ready to share with prospects.
2. You will have conclusions about the purpose of your church which will serve as a guideline for you and a source of information for prospects.

Reception and Evaluation of Material (30 min.)

Timing is a key factor in this session. Two alternatives have been presented to you about the gathering of material on your church and community. If the assignments were made as a part of the previous study session, this will be the first time the committee as a whole sees all the material. On the other hand, if a retreat was held when the Pastor Search Committee was first elected, then perhaps the material has already been in your hands.

Either way, you have the responsibility to evaluate the data gathered and determine what should be used. Using the guidelines in the study section, you can begin to put together a packet of information which will be as valuable to you

as a committee as it is to other persons who will be receiving it.

As you undertake this task you should do it with one overriding question: What is the purpose of our church? Not every bit of information you include will speak directly to that question, but it can be the determining factor in whether to include some material.

Correlation of Information (30 min.)

After you have evaluated information, you will want to go one step further. Take your church information and examine it in the light of the community it is supposed to serve. Does what you have found make sense?

Be realistic. For instance, if you find that your church has declined in attendance for the past five years, but the community it serves has grown steadily during that same period, then something is wrong. Don't start looking for excuses or reasons yet. For now, admit the reality of the truth you have discovered! Later, you or some other group may want to ask why.

What you cannot admit to yourselves will never be admitted to prospects; thus, they will not get as accurate a picture as they should. Be ruthless with your examinations and correlations. Where the specter is dim, accept it. Where the church shines, accept that and rejoice in it.

You may find that your church is like an island in its neighborhood because the majority of those attending drive from other neighborhoods. This should tell you and prospective pastors something about the future of the church.

As you do this correlating, if you find that a lot of things are out of sync, it is a good idea to take the time to write up your findings. A church which ministers well in its community need not do much elaborating.

Projection of Purpose (30 min.)

There are key times which a Pastor Search Committee should be very aware of during its term of work, and this is one of them. However, it is not a generally recognized key time.

The congregation doesn't expect this of you; the candidates will often be surprised but very pleased that you have done it; and you yourselves did not anticipate going this far. But now that you are in process, do it. Write a statement of purpose.

Translate all you have learned about the past, the present, and what appears to be the future of your church into a statement of purpose. Of course, it has to be the purpose of your church as your committee understands it. Everyone will understand that limitation.

Take the time now to have every member write a five-line paragraph which begins "The purpose of our church in this community is . . . ." Allow up to five minutes. After this is done, have each person read to the group. Within five minutes after all have read theirs, you should be able to write a con-

sensus statement. Remember, you are not trying to make a perfect theological statement for all churches—just an honest commentary on your church.

This leads naturally into some assignments.

Task 1: Place the responsibility for putting information about the church and community in final form for printing and distribution if this has not already been done.

Person responsible_____

Task 2: Allot the duty of writing up the decisions made concerning how the church is ministering in its community.

Person with the duty_____

Task 3: Constitute a subcommittee to share the statement of purpose with various segments of the church in order to get their responses as to its validity.

Persons constituted to serve____

_____

_____

Alternative Task: Designate a member of the committee to contact a cross section of the church membership (include all age groups) and ask them to write a one-page statement "I'm glad I live in ( ) because. . . ." This will be especially valuable if you become interested in a candidate who is not at all familiar with your community.

4

Contacting for Response

Study Session—What You Always Wanted to Know About Pastors But Were Afraid to Ask

Agenda:
Coming to grips with yourselves
Getting along in a strange land
Using your preparation to its maximum

Objectives:
At the conclusion of this session—
1. You will have examined your motives for seeking "someone else's pastor" and settled the matter for the balance of your tenure.
2. You will have attained a degree of confidence about interviewing which will enhance the immediate as well as future opportunities.

Coming to Grips with Yourselves (15 min.)

The day you go to hear a candidate preach and interview him should come only after each member of the committee has been able to rid himself of doubts of the appropriateness of the visit. This has several implications.

First of all, you should not go if you have reservations about the person being a worthy candidate for your church. Second, you should not go if the prospect is reticent about your presence on that Sunday. Third, you should realize

that if you have followed good methodology, you do not have to worry about "stealing" someone's pastor.

It may be helpful to go back and read some of the sections in the first chapters of the *Primer*. These cover the factors which indicate that a pastor who agrees to be a candidate is in reality inviting you to seek him out.

Getting Along in a Strange Land (15 min.)

Deception breeds deception. If you have been open in establishing a relationship to this point, why change? Remember that you are going with the pastor's approval and at least a tacit invitation.

There are few congregations large enough to worship with in complete anonymity. You will at least be recognized as strangers. Unless you are unfriendly, you will likely be put in the position of having to be deceitful if you insist on remaining unknown.

This is not advocacy of boisterousness, but a plea for common sense and good judgment. You can avoid sticking out in the crowd if you enter a few minutes before the service begins and sit in the middle of the auditorium. While you may not want to occupy a whole pew, there is nothing wrong with up to four people sitting together.

Since you will have set the time and

place for the interview prior to this date, the natural thing is to flow out with the crowd and go to. the appointed place. This allows you to be friendly, yet not be conspicuous by having to stand around for the crowd to leave.

Using Your Preparation to Its Maximum (60 min.)

You are not going to conduct an inquisition or to grill a suspect or to play "gotcha." The key word for the interview is single-mindedness. Everyone on the committee has worked until this point, and all need to keep working. However, there must be an understanding of the rules of the interview and an agreement to abide by them. It may be that you will want to review "Procedures for Conducting Interviews."

There has probably been some chafing at the bit since the methodology of this resource kit emphasizes a lot of preliminary work before the visiting of prospects begins. If the committee has sensed this, it should be emphasized that the time has arrived which all have been anticipating; therefore, good work must continue.

You should feel free to ask any questions which will help you know whether the prospect is God's choice for your church. But you will want to ask them kindly and with good taste.

It will help to keep in mind that this does not have to be the only interview, so some questions can wait. Since in almost every situation you will have some time limitations, you will concentrate on those inquiries which will help you to get a feel for his capability of helping you meet "the purpose of your church in its community." Establishing this as a positive possibility will enable you to know whether you want to ask

additional and more probing questions at a future time.

Appropriate types of questions are found at the end of this chapter. You will want to use your own words, but they illustrate the kinds of questions which will elicit helpful answers.

Assignments will be shared from the development session for this chapter. You may want to include the first section of it as a part of this meeting.

Procedures for Conducting Interviews

1. Schedule the interview—that is, make sure the prospective pastor knows you plan to do this as well as hear him preach.

2. Keep in mind that everyone will be somewhat nervous when the interview begins. Be cordial and have some brief and informal conversation.

3. Use the information you have received in recommendations, references, and personal data as a basis for the early discussions.

4. Gradually move from this level of discussion to more depth about the candidate's views of personal ministry and church organization and function. (See sample materials.)

5. Encourage the candidate to talk. Talk enough to keep direction and be friendly. (The committee should avoid getting into side conversations.) Avoid telling personal experiences that do not pertain to the purpose of the interview.

6. Ask questions that call for narrative statements rather than giving of opinions—for example, "Tell us how you work with the Sunday School," not "Do you think the Sunday School is important?"

7. Determine if you wish to ask doctrinal questions at this time. If so, make sure they are representative of the think-

ing of the whole church. State them carefully. If you are unsure of the response, probe further. However, do not press these matters to the point that the interview is ruined. You will have future opportunities to expand.

8. Listen to what he says; then ask follow-up questions. Notice what he does not say. Does he avoid some topics?

9. Be willing to answer questions. Give opportunity for this, and pay attention to what kinds of questions are asked.

10. Spend the last minutes of the interview recapping what has been discussed. Make sure the candidate knows *when* he can expect to hear from you. Have an understanding that this may be a note which terminates consideration or a contact which will extend the process if he is still interested.

Personal Ministry Questions

1. You will have opportunity to proclaim the gospel to believers and unbelievers. What are some ways you try to do this?

2. We see fellowship as an important part of our church. How would you use worship services, outreach programs, and the education programs to develop our fellowship?

3. Leadership is a basic need in our church. How do you relate to staff members, the deacon body, and the organizational leaders of a church? Tell us about your administrative skills.

4. Every church has persons in need. What are your approaches to hospital visitation, shut-ins, troubled people, etc.? How do you involve church members in ministering to one another?

Church Organization Questions

1. Briefly tell us about the program or-

ganizations of the church with which you have had the most experience in working.

2. How closely do you like to work with the Sunday School organization? Explain.

3. Of what importance are the mission organizations to the task of a church?

4. Tell us how the music program of a church can be used with the other programs.

5. Explain what kinds of training a church should provide its membership.

6. What other services would strengthen a church's ministry to its community?

When the Spouse Participates in the Interview

1. Be aware of her ability to relate to the group.

2. Ask how she gets her greatest fulfillment in Christian service.

3. Give her opportunity to ask questions at various points during the interview.

Additional Thoughts

You should be aware that many women are also completing seminary with degrees in music, education, and theology. For some of them, this is a way to supplement their husband's ministry. Others, however, would like to be considered as a part of the ministry team in a professional sense. An increasing number of women are candidates in their own right for pastoral positions.

Committees should be aware of this and seek to discover their own feelings before encountering such a situation. In the interview, attention should be given to the possibility of a husband/wife team if there are any indications that this is the desire of the couple.

Development Session—Conducting the Interview

Agenda:
   Finalizing the Logistics
   Doing the Interview
   Reviewing the Interview

Objectives:
   As you finish each section—
   1. You will feel comfortable with your interview arrangements.
   2. You will have added a new dimension to a pastor's life as well as your own lives.
   3. You will have begun the decision process about extending the relationship.

Finalizing the Logistics

If the committee chairperson is not a person given to detail, then another committee member should take the responsibility at this juncture. Keep in mind that the interview is not a business-as-usual situation; nor is it an optional task. Its importance demands strict preparation.

These questions must be answered:

1. Is the prospect fully aware that the committee will be present on this specific date?

2. Where is the church located? Do you know exactly how to get there and how long the trip will take?

3. If an overnight trip is involved, have reservations been made for lodging?

4. What is the starting time of the service you plan to attend?

5. Have arrangements been made for the postservice interview? Has the candidate's spouse been included?

6. Have arrangements been completed for the trip home so that families will know when to expect you?

Having solved these questions, you should appropriately make some further determinations. These will be in regard to what should be included in the agenda for the interview.

First, you will want to be aware that the service you attend is the first part of the interview. It is in monologue rather than dialogue, to be sure; but it is still an interview. You will want to be listening to and watching the candidate as he preaches. Content should be as carefully weighed as style.

At the same time you must be observant of how the rest of the people gathered at that service are responding to this person. Does he command their attention from the beginning? Is the attention held reasonably well? What type of open response does he seek to get from the congregation? Considering the approach, how do they respond?

You should gain some ideas from this part of the interview process which you can translate into questions at the regular interview which occurs later.

In what will ordinarily be an afternoon (though it often begins with lunch) interview session, you will accomplish what you plan to achieve and very little else.

This is why you will work out an agenda and determine how all committee members fit best in its intents and purpose. A possible agenda would include:
   Getting acquainted
   Review of mutual knowledge
   Basic questions by the committee
   Opportunity for questions by the prospect
   Overview of interview accomplishments
   Statement of future procedures

In most situations, the chairperson will take the lead in the first and last two items. If this is not to be the case, then the appropriate committee member will be designated.

The second item can be handled by a member of the committee who has the ability to condense information into a concise presentation. The two parts are "This is what we have learned about you—do you wish to add anything now or correct any information?" and "This is what we have shared about our church in the material we sent you—is this the understanding you had?"

Naturally, the prospect is going to have questions which come as a response to your questions. However, you should be careful to give the opportunity to have questions raised which are independent of the line of thought which you have chosen to pursue.

Doing the Interview

Your logistics and agenda go a large way toward circumscribing the interview process, but there are some further implications for your consideration.

Conduct the interview with a gentle spirit. Even if disagreements arise, this still does not justify conflict or anger. Sometimes disagreement is only a sign of misunderstanding which can be worked through. Even if it is more severe than that, the relationship does not have to be continued after the interview; so there is no need for censure of any sort.

Be willing to deal with tough issues. Finances are often put in this category. But this is a time of openness and honesty. Money, benefits, and expectations of commitment should not be avoided if they are natural to the interview. Usually the committee should take the initiative on these matters.

Have a sense of fair play. If this is not your first interview, don't take out on this prospect the prejudices and biases you developed from previous occasions. This is a different person and he deserves the right for you to assume that he does not possess the faults you have become wary of unless he shows you that he has them too.

Have an attitude of victory. Your victory may not be in finding this person to be God's choice for your church, but you can still be victorious. You can find triumph in doing a good job. You can have success in getting acquainted with another of God's ministers. These things can be rewarding in and of themselves. Yet all of the above may occur.

Reviewing the Interview

This is covered rather extensively in chapters 4 and 5 of the *Primer*. Still, here are some specific suggestions which will be beneficial.

If the committee is traveling together in one vehicle, take advantage of this and enter into immediate review. When the group is divided, this may still be possible; but the members should know in advance whether this will be the policy. When it is done, it should be in accordance with the guidelines of discussion adopted by the committee as a whole.

When a committee member has taken process notes (or minutes), these should be reproduced and distributed before the first committee meeting following the interview.

A very workable plan, whether or not extensive notes or minutes are available, is to use the interview agenda as a guide for the review. This will keep everyone together and offer an operable way to achieve evaluation in a reasonable time frame. Rehashing of certain reactions can be kept to a minimum.

In this review process you must face the decision as to whether the relationship will be continued. If the obvious consensus is negative, accept that and notify the prospect in the manner indicated in the *Primer*. A positive feeling can take on several means of continuing the relationship. Whatever the level, the prospect should be informed as to what the next step will be. The next chapter picks you up at this stage.

Assignments:

Task 1: Determine the person who handles details well and assign the logistical responsibilities.

      Person assigned_____

Task 2: Ascertain who has the ability to develop a concise review of mutual facts for presentation at the interview.

      Person chosen_____

Task 3: Stipulate who will cover the various areas of content of the interview questions.

      Person for_____

      Person for_____

Task 4: Discover who can take process notes (includes the flow of the session as well as the facts) or minutes of the interview for sharing with the whole committee.

      Person discovered_____

5

Handling the Turning Point

Study Session—Becoming Sensitive to the Need for Assurance

Agenda:
Arriving at a decision to continue a relationship
Acknowledging God's leadership
Accepting human responsibilities
According personal privileges

Objectives:
At the conclusion of this session—

1. You will have brought into proper perspective ways in which God leads at a time like this.

2. You will be willing to examine your committee's assumptions about the candidate and challenge them as needed.

3. You will be cognizant of the need for the candidate to expand the relationship before asking him for even preliminary commitment.

Arriving at a Decision to Continue a Relationship (60 min.)

After every visit and interview, a decision must be made as to whether you will remove the prospect from further contemplation or develop a deeper relationship. Sometimes this is done rather easily. All members feel the same way and are willing to openly express this feeling. This is true most often when the decision is negative.

When feelings are not as clear cut, more time is necessary to work through why this is so. Everyone should be encouraged to express the emotions which gave them the uncertain attitude. A negative or positive response may be the outcome of working through such uncertainty.

Sooner or later, a Pastor Search Committee does come to that time when they are certain that they have found God's choice for their church. Though it should not be so, committee members are quite surprised often to find they have second thoughts about whether this is really true.

Second thoughts lead to a turning point that a Pastor Search Committee works through with the next three steps.

Acknowledging God's Leadership (15 min.)

There are numerous times in the process of searching for a pastor when a committee collectively or individually wonders whether the Lord's leadership is involved. This happens because it is necessary to work on the human level as well as the spiritual. In the ebb and flow of this procedure, it sometimes seems that the task has become all human.

This is a time to stop and reflect upon

the very obvious times in which God has led and everyone has been aware of his special direction. Having participated in such sharing, it is appropriate that you pause and ask specifically for his continuing guidance. In a deep sense of trust, you should once again move to the point of acting in a responsible way to perform the tasks you have as a Pastor Search Committee.

Accepting Human Responsibilities
(15 min.)

Though the struggle with spiritual leadership may seem to be the greater burden, most committees actually experience more difficulties in being willing to work through human responsibilities.

The question of the moment is: "Are we comfortable with the idea of recommending this person, as a worthy candidate?" The answer is, "Probably not."

This occurs not because you have failed at any point prior to where you are now but because there is an intermediate step you need to follow which deepens assurance.

In the excitement of the realization that you are focusing in on a person who is not going to be an "ordinary" prospect, it is easy to gloss over questions and answers that are not as thorough as you had intended. These gnaw at your conscience for deeper consideration.

You also begin to realize that there needs to be more depth of relationship between the prime prospect and the committee. In all probability, you are experiencing the realization that the relationship has been one-sided and that it has been theoretical rather than practical.

There is a need for a deeper probing of whether this person and your church are meant for each other. The development session which follows will suggest ways of exploring this.

According Personal Privileges (15 min.)

While the Pastor Search Committee is having its gymnastic contemplations, the prospect is not sitting calmly, in ignorant bliss of his possible involvement.

To the contrary, until a committee expresses a negative feeling, most prospects will become emotionally involved in the consideration of a possible relationship. Part of this involvement is a multitude of questions which are raised in their minds and hearts about your church.

It is imperative that a Pastor Search Committee understand that pastoral prospects are experiencing the same ambivalent feelings they are. Is God leading? What about my family? Can I do the job? Do they really know me? What do I really know about them?

Just as a committee needs a strategy to get over their uncertainty, they must be sure the candidate also has such a pathway. Fortunately, there is a plan which satisfies both needs.

Getting ready for this plan includes these assignments (30 min.):

Task 1: The chairman contacts the prime prospect.

Task 2: All committee members write out questions which they feel need further coverage. One person is selected to edit the lists.

Person selected_____

Task 3: Assign a committee member to check the church calendar for weekend events for the next four to six weeks. It is often advisable to check school and community calendars also.

Person assigned_____

Development Session—Decision Time: Shall We Continue or Cease Relationships?

Agenda:
  Putting forth a limited invitation
  Participating in a different kind of interview
  Pulling together a consensus decision

Objectives:
  At the conclusion of this session—
  1. You will have had an "on-the-field" interview with your primary candidate.
  2. You will have explored all matters which have been unanswered in the minds of the committee or the candidate.
  3. You will have reached a decision which has been reinforced by strategies for implementation.

Putting Forth a Limited Invitation

"God's choice for our church" is what you are thinking, but you want to be sure. How can you be sure? Absolute certainty will only come by acknowledgment of the congregation, but the committee can act in a way which will help immensely.

Invite the prospect to visit your church field. This is a confidential visit and is not publicized. It is a visit based upon a limited invitation.

Your telephone call to the prospect will be something of this nature: "We believe that God has led us to you, and we want to go further in our relationship. If you believe God might be in this, we would like to have you visit our church field on a weekday in the near future. There is no obligation on either of us at this point, though we definitely feel that there might be a commitment by the end of this special visit and interview. Are you (and your mate) willing to come under such an arrangement?"

A positive response should mean that a date is set and the visit is arranged. Suggestions about the logistics of the visit are found at the end of this chapter under the title "From a Responsive Interview to a Possible Call."

Participating in a Different Kind of Interview

In the first interview with the prospect, you were carrying out general explorations. Now you want to probe designated matters. These will include:
  1. Specific questions from the first interview which the committee has agreed need more consideration.
  2. New questions which have arisen in the light of the person being considered a serious prospect.
  3. Sharing of new information which is relevant because of the advanced relationship, the fact of being on the church field, or both.
  4. The three matters previously listed from the candidate's viewpoint.

Your purpose in this session is to nail down where everybody stands. Openness and honesty must prevail. To evade issues at this point is to leave the committee or the candidate with unresolved feelings and thus to defeat the whole purpose of the engagement. Such issues include financial matters, privileges of time (vacations, revivals, continuing education, etc.), clarification of doctrinal stance, and clearing the air about nagging small misunderstandings.

As these matters are worked through and the committee still has positive feelings, there should be a gradual shift to topics related to an official visit which includes appearing "in view of a call." Studying the next chapter will enable you to know what details need to be worked out between the committee and prospect.

Pulling Together a Consensus Decision

Normally by this stage of negotiation a committee does not get too many surprises. However, if you do, and if the surprise is negative and serious, the Pastor Search Committee should call a halt to the interview and in the spirit of kindness let the candidate return home. Being coy and continuing a charade when the group knows the interest is gone is not an act of kindness.

When this interview serves as an affirmation to previous positive progress, it should be concluded with several actions.

First, if the church has other full-time staff members, there should be a meeting arranged between them and the prospect. This will take extra time but is worth it. The committee should get feedback from the meeting(s); and if there is significant negative reaction of any kind, take this into consideration. Review the suggestions about this in the *Primer*.

Second, discuss what will be done when the prospect comes before the church at the official invitation of the committee. Make sure all elements of the visit are understood and agreed upon.

Third, talk about dates. Don't rush the date for the official visit. Pick out the best weekend available in a reasonable time, not the first one that can be squeezed in. When this visit is concluded, it will necessitate the following assignments:

Task 1: Enlist a committee member to research matters which are discussed but need further study and to furnish the findings to the candidate and remainder of the committee.

Person enlisted_____

Task 2: If the chairperson's work

schedule makes it difficult to communicate with him at times, choose another person from the committee to serve as liaison with the candidate in the interim before the official visit.

Person chosen_____

From a Responsive Interview to a Possible Call

It may be the first, third, or tenth time that the committee hears a person preach and interviews him, but the time always comes when a committee "knows" they want to expand and extend the relationship.

Following guidelines through this experience will keep misunderstanding at a minimum and the relationship progressing.

1. Never make a commitment during a first interview other than that the prospect will hear within a certain period concerning the committee's decision regarding him.

2. When the decision is positive, contact the person as soon as possible to receive his response to the possibility of pursuing the matter further. If he is secure in wanting to explore the situation further, set a date for him and his spouse to visit the church field (providing the distance is not prohibitive).

3. This is still a confidential situation between the committee and the prospect. The visit to the field should be done in relative obscurity with only one or two committee members present at a time. After driving about the community and showing church facilities and records, have a private night meeting with the committee as a whole.

4. If the committee and the prospect are in basic agreement that the process should continue, arrange a confidential meeting with the professional staff, probably for the next morning.

5. At the conclusion of that meeting,

come to an agreement as to when the candidate can come before the church. Be sure to check dates to avoid holidays, etc.

6. Discuss the type of moving arrangements which would be used. Avoid asking the pastor to move under conditions which would endanger his family or even his belongings. You are calling him to come to stay; invest accordingly.

7. When the couple is ready to return to their present home, hand them a check (in an envelope) covering all expenses of the trip not previously paid by the church. Also remember that he will have to pay a supply for his own pulpit. Assure them that the future visit will also be cared for in like manner.

8. Communicate by telephone at least one time between this visit and the "in-view-of-a-call visit." Write a letter outlining all agreements as understood by your committee.

9. Notify the church membership of the date of the announcement of the prospective pastor's identity.

10. Begin to use appropriate bulletin inserts.

6

Wrapping Up the Job

Study Session—A Twofold Approach to Satisfaction

Agenda:
Elements of a well-done presentation
of a candidate
Factors that influence a happy pastor-
people relationship

Objectives:
At the conclusion of this session—
1. You will have a knowledge of what should be included in the plans for the presentation of your pastoral candidate.
2. You will have begun to think about the seemingly small matters which often make the difference in a new person's ability to become "pastor."

Development Session—Completing Your Task in a Commendable Manner

Agenda:
Constructing a full strategy of
presentation
Applying the finishing touches

Objectives:
At the conclusion of this session—
1. You will be prepared to present your candidate to the congregation in a way that is fair to all concerned and will ensure an equitable decision.
2. You will know exactly what steps you still need to take according to the congregation's decision about the call.

Elements of a Well-done Presentation of a Candidate (60 min.)

This is another of those pivotal times for the Pastor Search Committee. You can fall back on the traditional methods of pulpit committees and still succeed in having the person called as pastor. Keep in mind, however, that the more you do, the more you will benefit the church and the candidate.

First, go back to the chapters on communication in this book and the *Primer.* Study the sections that relate to presentation of the candidate and put those ideas to good use.

Then you will want to discuss how the Pastor Search Committee is going to be specifically involved in the presentation process.

This is no time for a low profile. The committee will want to be bold and open at all times. Your very presence with an optimistic spirit will give the congregation added assurance that you have done a good job and are excited about the future.

Finally, be sure to use the presentation checklist at the end of this chapter.

Factors that Influence a Happy Pastor-People Relationship (60 min.)

Not every church is going to be influenced by the same determinants when the pastor and the people are getting acquainted. There are some which seem to have more bearing than others, particularly in the early stages of acquaintance. Most of these evolve around the congregation's sense of equal opportunity in getting to know the candidate.

The Pastor Search Committee needs to work very hard to provide every member of the congregation with the privilege of becoming personally acquainted with the prospective pastor. The fact that every person will not take advantage of this is not important. Knowing that the opportunity was there will be etched in their memories much longer than the fact that they failed to avail themselves of the right.

It is a devastating blow to future relationships for some people in the congregation to be put in a second-class-citizen situation. This is never the intent, of course; but it does happen when a portion (deacons, for instance) of the body is invited to a special meeting with the candidate and the rest must wait until the Sunday services. Make sure that your plans for introducing a prospect before Sunday include the whole church body.

If a church group has the right to have an intervening relationship between the Pastor Search Committee and the whole church when a pastor is being called, then it is certain that they will always feel they have that right after the pastor is called. Nothing should be done to damage the direct relationship between pastor and people.

Another step the committee will want to take is to show itself and the church as a whole to be a caring people. Often, the week after a call has been issued, the pastor-to-be becomes somewhat of a forgotten person. Regular contact should be maintained to assure that the transition process will go smoothly.

You will also want to continue to inform the church about the details of welcoming a new pastor. While some in the church may scoff at this as being old hat, you need to stick to your plans and encourage the excitement which the majority feel.

Assignments will be made at the end of the development session.

The Presentation of the Prospective Pastor to the Congregation

1. Set the date with the prospect, making sure that the time agreed upon does not place him or the church under a handicap.

2. Once the date has been set, make a public announcement at the next Sunday morning worship service. Do not tell any "special" individuals or groups before the congregation is told. Announce when the vote will be taken, and continue to stress this point.

3. In the next edition of church news (newsletter or Sunday bulletin), give a complete biographical sketch of the person to be recommended. If there is an extended time before he is to come, repeat the announcement and sharing of this information.

4. Plan to have the prospective pastor and family on the church field for at least two days with a carefully planned schedule.

   (a) Reserve appropriate rooms and service for the family.

   (b) Have carefully planned tours of the community if this has not been done previously.

   (c) Show all church facilities if this is the first visit.

60

(d) Arrange for introduction to all staff members if not already acquainted. In any event, give time for private discussions with staff.

(e) Plan an open meeting for early Saturday evening when the whole church is invited. The size of the congregation will determine the type of gathering. The purpose is to give the prospect and the church an opportunity to get acquainted before the "trial sermon."

(f) At the service when the prospective pastor is to preach (usually AM), the committee chairperson should give a warm introduction as early in the service as possible.

(g) When possible, have the candidate preach again at the evening service. This would then be the most appropriate time for the congregation to vote unless prohibited by church policy.

(h) Announce the vote to the church and the prospect as soon as counted. Do not place artificial limitations upon the vote in advance.

(i) If the vote is to call, give the person adequate time to give a decision to the church.

(j) Upon receiving an answer, announce it to the whole church and move to completing the task of the committee.

Terminating Your Work as a Committee

This is as important for the continuing happiness of the pastor, the committee, and the church as a whole as anything you will do during your tenure of service.

First, you will want to be sure that any agreements made within the church, its committees, and the new pastor are thoroughly understood by all. Besides all of this being reviewed at the time of the call, it should be repeated in the announcements and explanations made regarding acceptance and moving schedule.

Second, you will oversee the orderly carrying out of the relocating of the new pastor and his family. This involves these steps:

(1) Proper contact with the parties responsible for the moving. This is based upon principles worked out before the call.

(2) Preparation of facilities. If a parsonage is owned, make sure it is in top condition. If a housing allowance is used, double-check with utility companies, etc. In either case have the study/office clean and ready.

(3) Have the necessary number of church members available to provide meals, child care, etc.

(4) Provision for first night in motel if necessary.

Third, plan the first Sunday services in conjunction with the new pastor and the approval of the congregation.

(1) Sunday morning is a Covenant Service, the purpose being to very positively bind the will, direction, and commitment of pastor and people to work together for a reasonable duration.

(2) Sunday evening prior to the regular worship service should be a form of "Meet the Pastor in Dialogue." Have guidelines which restrict opinion but give opportunity for explaining direction of ministry.

(3) For the Sunday evening worship service, ask the pastor to preach on "My Future as a Minister" or "The Future Church as I See It."

(4) Conclude the day with a reception for the pastor and family.

Fourth, arrange a meeting for the following day between the Pastor Search

Committee and the Pastor.

(1) "Pastor, we are glad you are here."

(2) "We want you to pastor the whole church."

(3) "We are not the whole church or the most important members."

(4) "Call on us individually as you would any other church member, but we are no longer the Pastor Search Committee."

(5) "Let's pray for our church."

Fifth, use the bulletin inserts on appropriate Sundays.

Constructing a Full Strategy of Presentation

Up until very recently, you have been thinking about and comparing several people. Now is the time to focus completely on one person. You want to do your best to help the average church member know as much about the person you believe to be God's choice for your church as you do.

This will involve reviewing communication plans. Unless you have a very extensive system of weekly communication, a special letter such as the sample at the end of this chapter should be used. You may want to use it anyway.

Take seriously every item on the ten-stage presentation guide at the end of this chapter. You never know which effort will be the one which will get the attention of a church member. On the other hand, it is ordinarily the cumulative effect which ultimately achieves your goal of a truly informed congregation.

You would do well to keep in mind that only a truly informed congregation will make a decision that you can accept after all of your hard work. This will be true even when the remote possibility of a negative vote results.

Applying the Finishing Touches

If the congregation votes to call the person you have recommended, your task is on the final road to completion. You now should inform the congregation on the following matters.

1. When can an answer be expected?

Some prospects are prepared to give an answer as soon as the call is extended. If this is so, tell the people.

Others want time for further consideration. The committee should ask for a specific time by which they can expect an answer. With all the efforts which have gone before the vote, it would take unusual circumstances to justify more than one week.

2. What should we expect in the coming weeks?

As soon as an answer is received, the committee should work out the details of the move and share them with the congregation (this has been tentatively done in the period of negotiation).

In addition, the committee will also want to use the bulletin inserts and other media to prepare the congregation to accept the new pastor as rapidly as possible.

3. How can we be involved?

The bulletin inserts help here also. In the *Primer* there are suggestions for involvement which you should review.

4. Why is your job over?

This may not be a question the people of the church will ask, but you should answer it for them anyway. In the rare situations where a negative vote is received, the Pastor Search Committee responsibilities are naturally different.

First, you have the responsibility for telling the congregation and the candidate. In all probability, there should be no speculation as to why this occurred.

Second, you should inform the congregation within a week's time of your intentions as a committee. Unless you have strong reason not to do so, the committee should continue. A new committee will mean a complete new process.

The New Pastor's First Sunday

Often this is a very ordinary or perhaps below-ordinary Sunday. There are reasons why this occurs. Sometimes the pastor moves early in the week and begins to fall into routine type of work and puts no special focus on Sunday. With others, the move is made at the very end of the week, and fatigue affects him that first Sunday.

The move should be made early in the week, but your committee should plan with the church and the pastor for his first ministry responsibilities to be on Sunday and for it to be a special day.

In the resource kit is an outline of a Covenant Service for the Sunday morning service. In the *Primer* are ideas for an evening with special emphasis on beginning the establishment of relationships. Doing these things can make it a day to remember.

When you carry through on the termination plans outlined in the resource sheet which follows then:

"Congratulations are in order for a job well done!"

Assignments:

Task 1: Determine what each committee member is going to do in a specific act to have a visible role in the presentation process.

Roles determined_____

_____

_____

_____

_____

_____

_____

Task 2: Early in preparation for presentation have a person write a draft of the formal recommendation which the committee will make to the church. In subsequent meetings, this can be edited by the total committee.

Person to write_____

Task 3: Choose other people of the church who can ably be involved in the first Sunday services and activities and enlist their support.

People chosen_____

_____

_____

_____

_____

_____

_____

SAMPLE LETTER TO CHURCH MEMBERSHIP

September 25, 1979

Dear Church Family,

Some months ago you elected us to one of the most important committees our church will ever have. We have tried to be faithful to the task you gave us.

It is with great joy and anticipation that we announce to you that we have invited Rev. Paul Luther to officially be in our church (in view of a call to become our pastor) on Sunday, October 10.

You will find in the enclosed material valuable information about his ministry experience and his personal background. Included also is an exact copy of the recommendation which will be brought to the congregation.

In order that you may have the opportunity to become personally acquainted with him, we have invited Rev. Luther and his family to be present for an informal time with the whole church family at 7:00 PM on Saturday, October 9. Details will be in the church newsletter.

Please continue to pray with us through the coming weeks as you have during these past months.

Sincerely,

Your Pastor Search Committee

_____   _____
_____   _____
_____   _____
_____   _____

P.S. We are truly excited because we believe we have found God's choice for our church.

enc: Biographical data
     Copy of recommendation